500

Essential Sites for

SMART SURFERS

D1350673

Series Editor: Colleen Collier
Research: Jodie Geddes
Contributors: Jane Purcell, Gareth Tuppenney, Jane Smith,
Roya Ireland, Christine Pountney, Richard Skinner
Page Design and Layout: Linley Clode
Cover Design: Sol Communications Ltd

Published by:
Lagoon Books
PO Box 311, KT2 5QW, UK
PO Box 990676, Boston, MA 02199, USA

www.lagoongames.com

ISBN: 1-902813-28-6

© Lagoon Books, 2000
Lagoon Books is a trademark of
Lagoon Trading Company Limited.

All rights reserved.

All rights reserved. No part of this publication
may be reproduced, stored in a retrieval system, or
transmitted in any form or by any other means, electronic,
mechanical, photocopying or otherwise, without
prior permission in writing from the publisher.

Printed in Singapore.

500
Essential Sites for
SMART SURFERS

LAGOON
BOOKS

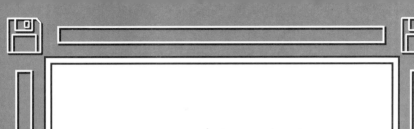

While every care has been taken to ensure
the material in this book is accurate at
the time of press, the constantly changing
nature of the Internet makes it impossible
to guarantee that every address will be
correct or every web site available.

Every effort will be made to revise and
update sites on our web site.

Lagoon will assume neither liability nor
responsibility to any person or entity with
respect to any loss, damage or suitability of
the web sites contained in this book.

CONTENTS

INTRODUCTION

"The Internet is a tidal wave...drowning those who don't learn to swim in its waves" – Bill Gates

Over the past few years, many guides to the Internet have been written explaining how to access the Net and how to use it. But now everyone's looking for a fun and easy-to-use guide to the best sites, so here it is!

This stunning 288-page directory lists 500 Essential Sites for Smart Surfers, and is subdivided into six amazing chapters according to subject to make searching even easier!

The research has been carried out by an avid team of fun-loving Internet surfers, whose brief was to find the best sites on the Web for you to enjoy – which is just what they did! Go to p84 or p169 to see what I mean!

Each site is listed with the web address and several lines of text, hinting at what you might find if you log on and visit the web site. The book is for surfers of all ages and abilities – you don't have to be a computer whizz or Internet expert to use it.

Amongst the 500 fantastic web sites listed here, you will be able to find out...

...How to make a million dollars
...Where to find your missing socks
...Where to purchase the very latest in hi-tech gadgets and gizmos
...Where to get hold of fake celebrity driver's licenses
...How to find a sponsor for your personal webpage
...How to become a gambling expert
...The latest sport news, deals and scores
...Where you can buy a top-of-the-range Lamborghini

It's amazing what people put on the Internet, so here is the ultimate guide to finding all that is exciting, innovative, attainable and fantastical!

Get online for hours of fun and entertainment!

If it's new and exciting, you'll find it here!

1

LIFESTYLE

Time to Quit?
http://www.quitsmokingsupport.com

It's now March, and you still haven't
followed through with that New Year's
resolution! Get all the support you need
to quit at this helpful web site.

Agony Uncle
http://www.agony-uncle.com

If you're too embarrassed to write into
a magazine problem page let Agony
Uncle come to the rescue! Simply email
him and he will advise you soon after.

5

Nothing to Wear?
**http://www.geocities.sunsetstrip/
towers/6612/outfit.htm**

This clever chart will solve daily dressing
dilemmas! Questions to answer include
'Is it clean?' and then you may be
asked to do the 'smell test'.

Healthy Ideas
http://www.healthyideas.com

This site features practical and modern
advice for the millennium woman, listed
in useful sections such as food, health,
and romance.

Safe Sex
http://www.condoms4u.com

Everything you need to know about condoms! Whatever size or color you're after, this excellent site will answer your queries and make sex both safe and fun.

Food Labels
http://www.na1.usda.gov/ 8001/py/pmap.htm

If the bizarre ingredients on your food labels look like they need an interpreter, this site will help you. Warning – reading this may cause you to lose your appetite!

Cyber Chicks
http://www.match.com

Maybe you are ready to consider sharing your life with someone! Too serious? Register with this site and meet people who could turn out to be good friends or maybe the love of your life.

Diet Watch
http://www.dietwatch.com

This is a Web-based support group for those who haven't found losing weight very easy. Share your tips and feelings online with others in the same position.

Muscle Man
http://www.muscle-fitness.com

Stop staring at the computer screen and take some action! – but first, check out the exercise regime at this site and soon you could look like Schwarzenegger.

Help is at Hand
http://www.alcoholismhelp.com

Fed up feeling like you've crashed head on with a juggernaut? Take action by visiting a site that helps you take a close look at your drinking habits without the usual moralizing.

Hypochondriac Heaven
http://www.intellihealth.com

Be honest! When your nose is running, do you automatically think you have flu? Does a slight headache mean your brain tumor has returned? If you are a bit of a hypochondriac, this online medical site will give you unbiased medical advice.

Cyberdiet
http://www.cyberdiet.com

This is a well-organized site with lots of sensible advice on following a healthy eating plan – long-term moderation with exercise!

Swoon!
http://www.swoon.com

Log on here and take the quiz to find out all about yourself – then read the daily horoscopes and find out who your ideal love match is!

Smile!
http://www.ada.org/tc-cons.html

The first thing people notice when they meet you is your smile. To ensure your pearly whites are ready to be scrutinized, check out this dental hygiene site first!

Viagra Boys
http://www.pfizer.com

This user-friendly and informative site gives you the low-down on Viagra, and also lots of other useful information on health issues and sexual problems.

12

Health Check
http://www.youfirst.com

Sometimes life becomes so busy you neglect your most important asset – You! This enormous site offers a health assessment test so that you can tell what needs fixing!

Allergy Info
http://www.allergy-info.com

If summer for you means misery, check this site out for the A–Z of allergies. If you can't find an answer, it will simply direct you to a site that can.

Drugstore Cowboy
http://www.drugstore.com

Whether you're suffering from cold and flu, or you snore like a wild hog, consult this online pharmacy for medical advice and supplies.

Illness Support Group
http://www.mediconsult.com

If you are suffering from an illness and feel that no one understands what you are going through, click on to this medical site and meet others in a similar predicament.

Micro Magic Carpet
http://www.expedia.msn.com

The Microsoft travel web site, bursting
with information about the places
you've been dreaming of visiting, and
lots of tips on how to get there.

Crazy Dog
http://www.infomatch.com/~cdtg

Let 'Crazy Dog' help you decide what
to pack, how to budget, and even how
to choose a backpack to put it all in!
Don't leave home without consulting
him first.

The Zoo
http://www.travelzoo.com

Think of this zoo as a protector against man-eating travel beasts, such as ridiculously high airfares! A one-stop travel shop, this site will give you the best fares and deals.

Rough Job!
http://travel.roughguides.com

This Rough Guide site details over 6,000 travel destinations and gives you information, like where to find a doctor at 2.00 am in Lahore!

City Guide
http://www.cnn.com/travel/city.guides

Wandering around a new city looking bewildered is a sure-fire way to get mugged! Get wise and plan ahead by downloading a city map of the place you are about to visit.

Sound Advice
http://www.thebackpacker.net

If you're going to plan each day as it comes on your overseas travels, keep some of the useful pointers featured at this site at the back of your mind.

Know Thy Country
http://www.newsd.com

If you want to know more about the
country you are intending to visit, take a
look at this site that features over 8,300
worldwide publications.

Top 40
http://www.infoplease.com/
spot/traveldest.html

Head to this great site that lists the top
40 travel destinations this year. You can't
go wrong!

Border Control
http://www.customs.treas.gov

Have a chat to the customs department
of the country you are planning to visit.
A good way to determine if that bottle
of whisky you are taking over the border
is legal!

Fodor's Guide
http://www.fodors.com

The Fodor Guide mini-books are very
useful for city travel, so check them out
at this stylish web site.

Business Travel
http://www.msnbc.com/ modules/travel/toolkit.asp

It's often hard to plan a business trip away, but at least the company has to pay for it! Learn how to make the most of business travel at this useful online toolkit.

Expense Account
http://www.biztravel.com

Go and book the best in business travel luxury at this online travel agency that is geared towards hot executives just like you!

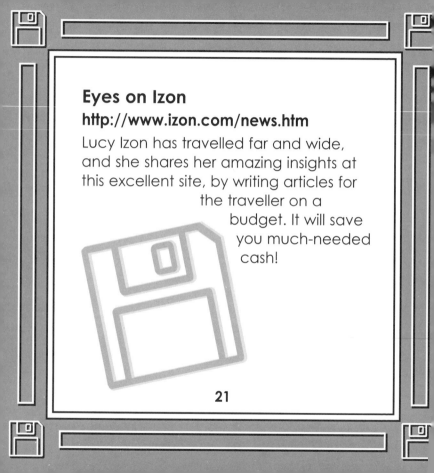

Eyes on Izon
http://www.izon.com/news.htm

Lucy Izon has travelled far and wide, and she shares her amazing insights at this excellent site, by writing articles for the traveller on a budget. It will save you much-needed cash!

Ultimate City
http://www.ci.nyc.ny.us

Read up on the city that never sleeps,
New York, before you even leave home
at this web site, full of practical advice.

Email Me!
**http://www.netcafeguide.com/
frames.html**

This site contains listings of more than
2,700 Internet cafes to make sure your
travel news gets back quickly to your
family.

Last Minute
http://www.lastminute.com

This much-fêted site is excellent for spontaneous trips and tickets – simply log on for last minute deals on flights, packages and accommodation.

Free Flights!
http://www.frequentflier.com

The best way to fly is for free, and this cool site explains all you need to know about frequent flyer points and how to claim them.

23

Have Laptop, Will Travel
http://www.roadnews.com

Can't bear to part with your beloved laptop even on vacation? Visit here for the low-down on keeping it in tip-top condition on the road.

Harbor View
http://www.viewsydney.com

This web-cam has been set up at a location on the harbor in Sydney, Australia. If you tire of gazing at the Opera House, change the view!

Cyber Embassy
http://www.embpage.org

Check all your visa requirements at your
local embassy online – a useful way to
avoid having to stand in line for hours!

Language Net
http://www.travlang.com

An excellent site for the roving traveller
to pick up a few basic phrases for use in
40 countries. Arm yourself with handy
phrases such as 'Where is the railway
station?'

25

Cyber Embassy
http://www.embpage.org

Check all your visa requirements at your
local embassy online – a useful way to
avoid having to stand in line for hours!

Language Net
http://www.travlang.com

An excellent site for the roving traveller
to pick up a few basic phrases for use in
40 countries. Arm yourself with handy
phrases such as 'Where is the railway
station?'

Have Laptop, Will Travel
http://www.roadnews.com

Can't bear to part with your beloved laptop even on vacation? Visit here for the low-down on keeping it in tip-top condition on the road.

Harbor View
http://www.viewsydney.com

This web-cam has been set up at a location on the harbor in Sydney, Australia. If you tire of gazing at the Opera House, change the view!

Railroading
http://www.trainweb.com/travel

Often the best and most peaceful way to travel is by train. So check this site out for travel times and fares, and then hit the rails and relax as the scenery passes by.

Native Travel
http://www.vtourist.com

Paying for cabs in most major cities will have you wiring home for money before you've even reached the hotel! Check out the local transport at this site and save loads of money!

Experience Oz
http://www.ozexperience.com

Experience Australia at this fantastic site
that reveals the best trips 'down under'.
Imagine a trip through the Outback and
watching sunrise over Ayers Rock!

Great Deals!
http://www.istc.org

Still young enough to be a student?
Then sign up to this discount scheme site
and enjoy cut-price deals to all major
destinations.

By Travellers, For Travellers
http://www.travel-library.com

This great site allows you to log on and read other people's accounts of countries you may shortly be visiting.

High Octane
http://www.adventure-mag.com

Take the plunge and organize that bungee-jumping week away. This online mag details the best adventure vacations around!

Gastronomic Traveller
http://uk.curryguide.com

A mouth-watering site dedicated to
wonderful Indian food in Britain – check
out the recipes and the best restaurants.

Real Ale
**http://www.geocities.com/
southbeach/pier/4076/beer.html**

A site that allows you to learn how to
brew your own ale! It also has a listing of
all the different types, so I guess it's
educational too!

Dinner Fiasco
http://www.mealsforyou.com

The dinner party that was for four has suddenly turned into a medieval banquet! Click on this brilliant dinner site and let them custom-make the recipe and cooking agenda for you!

Guinness
http://www.guinness.ie

The official Guinness web site in Ireland, dedicated to all lovers of the dark and frothy ale. Everything comes to he who waits!

Oktoberfest
http://www.bier.de/beer.html

Any country that dedicates an entire month to beer, sausage and lederhosen must have a great sense of humor. Check out the German party animals at this site!

Hemingway's Tipple
http://bob.bob.bofh.org/absinthe

This site gives a step-by-step guide to concocting one of the most lethal drinks known to man, namely Absinthe. It is illegal in some countries, so maybe just reading about it is safer!

Global Gourmet
http://www.globalgourmet.com

A visual feast from all over the globe, containing excellent pointers and easy-to-follow recipes.

Simply Food
http://www.simplyfood.com

Next time ten unexpected guests turn up for dinner, log on to this fantastic site that is filled with hundreds of recipes, and design and layout ideas for the table.

Le Banquet
http://www.frenchwinesfood.com

Click on to this site for a low-down on frogs legs, snails and fantastic wine. If you love French food, this is the place for you!

Vino Vino
http://www.winespectator.com

If you want to know what to do when the waiter asks you to taste the wine, visit this site – it's an entire ezine dedicated to wine tasting.

Cheese and Wine
http://www.cheese.com

Cheese – the perfect accompaniment to your favorite claret. You won't believe the variety mentioned at this site dedicated to the world's best cheese.

Dinner is Served
http://food.epicurious.com

An amazing site that contains thousands of quick-and-easy recipes for every occasion, and it also contains lots of links to other great food sites.

Cocktail Hour
http://www.idrink.com

An excellent site to visit if you are organizing a cocktail party. It lists over 5,000 wild, wacky, and often head-spinning drink recipes to complement your party atmosphere.

Kosher
http://www.kosherinfo.com

If you only eat Kosher food, but are unsure where to obtain it in a new city, log on to this helpful site.

No Carrots Here!
http://www.southroad.freeserve.co.uk/altfood.htm

You won't find many Hollywood actresses logging on to this site, but if low-calorie health food turns you off, click on to this site full of naughty nibbles!

Food Channel
http://www.foodchannel.com

Feast your eyes on this web page
crammed full of mouth-watering
information for food lovers everywhere.

Recipes For Love
http://soar.berkeley.edu/recipes/

Need to impress a dinner guest, but only
have last night's pizza? Before you pick
up the phone to order another, log onto
this site and download a spectacular
recipe guaranteed to impress!

Around the Globe
http://www.tubears.com

Visit this tasty site containing more than 50,000 recipes to entice even the most jaded palate. With delicious recipes from around the world, there'll be no excuse for ordering take-away food ever again!

Recipe Exchange
http://www.recipexchange.com

Swap cooking disaster stories and tips online at this site that positively encourages you to participate.

Hot Buttered Recipes
http://www.classicrecipes.com

Jam-packed with user-friendly cookery tips for all culinary types. If you want to share your Grandma's Apple Pie recipe with the entire Internet baking populous, simply type it in!

Organics
http://www.organicsdirect.com

If the only food you touch is organic,
you'd better log on to this natural site
where you can buy fresh, organic
produce online.

Carnivore
http://www.meatmatters.com

Get stuck into this juicy site, filled to the
brim with meaty recipes, nutritional
advice, and cute pictures of dancing
sausages! Not for faint-hearted
vegetarians.

Quackers
http://www.quackwatch.com

This site's aim is to 'combat health-related frauds, myths, fads, and fallacies'. If you are suffering from an illness, check this site to determine if treatments you have heard of are real or fake!

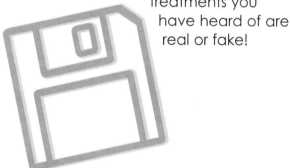

Veggie Gourmet
http://www.vegweb.com

Vegetarian cooking made deliciously easy at this fun and accessible site! Your culinary expertise need no longer consist of vegetables smothered in cheese!

Kindergarten Chef
http://www.learn2.com/browse/food.html

Isn't it time you learned to stop slaving over a tin opener and actually learn the basics of cooking? This excellent site for beginners will have you making 'Coq au Vin' in no time!

Rabbit Food
http://www.saladrecipes.com

You can't go wrong with a fresh, crunchy salad to accompany the summer barbecue, so learn how to make a seriously good alternative to a mere bowl of lettuce at this healthy site.

Why?
http://whyfiles.news.wisc.edu

Featuring the 'science behind the news', this web site hosts debates and features articles on current health and news issues to put you in the know.

Move It!
http://www.justmove.org

You don't have to run 20 kilometers a day according to this health-conscious site – they just want you to move and provide tips and advice to get you started!

Fast Facts
http://www.refdesk.com

Need some facts at your fingertips fast? Log on to this vast reference site that aims to provide you with all the answers in a hurry.

46

Red Roses
http://www.1001waystoberomantic.com

Put a sparkle back into your loved one's
eyes by checking out this site dedicated
to 'cool, creative, wonderful and wacky
romantic ideas' to help keep the
passion alive.

Feet off the Table!
http://www.etiquette-network.com

Take the online 'Table Manners' test and an 'Image Test' at this polite site to determine if you desperately need help with etiquette. Then read the tips and advice.

Be Well
http://www.bewell.com

Improve your health and lifestyle immediately by clicking on to this web site that is full of advice for men, women and children.

Work Abroad
http://www.overseasjobs.com

Take advantage of unique opportunities by spending time working abroad. At this international employment site, you can search for the job of your dreams.

2

MONEY, MONEY, MONEY

Who Wants to be a Millionaire?
**http://abc.go.com/
primetime/millionaire/mill_hme.html**

You do? Join the line, or else log on to this site that highlights the joy of previous contestants on this top-rating TV show!

Kitchen Table Millionaire
http://www.windandsea.com

Whether you're stuck for 'the idea', or simply need help setting off down the road of entrepreneurship, this online guidebook will give you a head start.

Armchair Millionaire
http://www.armchairmillionaire.com/

Want a head start on the road to fortune? Then log on here for tips on where to start and how to maintain long-term vision.

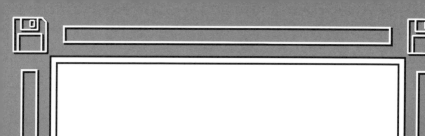

Read All About It
**http://www.randomhouse.com/
features/millionairekit/**

This book by Stephen L Nelson outlines
strategies and tips on saving, insurance
and investment, and tells you how easy
it is to earn one million bucks.

My CFO
http://www.mycfo.com

The customized services at this site will help you manage, build and preserve your wealth.

Richest Americans
http://www.forbes.com/ tool/toolbox/rich400/

Access 'The Forbes Four Hundred' database and find the names of all the men in Florida with net worths over one billion dollars – the truly choosy can search by age and marital status!

Financial Support
http://www.thebrainstormers.com/

Have you invented something you just
know will be an overnight success, but
can't afford the money for marketing it?
Look no further…

Gutter to Glitter
**http://www.usdreams.com/
dejoria5051.html**

An inspiring story of one man's leap from
homelessness to playboy millionaire! It
didn't happen overnight, but it did
happen!

Bake Until Golden…Rich!
http://www.geocities.com/ bourbonstreet/4968/sweetgj01.html

The proof is in the pudding! This site suggests that all it takes to make a million is the following recipe – mix crackers, condensed milk and lemon juice…bake at 40 degrees and…voila!

The Language of Money
http://www.investorwords.com

If your financial vocabulary is a bit rusty but you still want to impress your friends, this is the site to visit to find out the difference between an open and closed-end fund.

Spamscam
http://www.junkemail.org

'Spamscam' is the official name for
email fraud – check this site on how to
report it and what Bills are being passed
to prevent it.

Classic Cars
http://www.stlouiscarmuseum.com/

Whether you think you can afford one or
not, this is a fun site to view everything
from carriages to hot-rods – you can also
see which celebs have shopped here
too!

News
http://finance.uk.yahoo.com

All the latest information you need on the complete world of finance.

Plastic Fantastic
http://www.via.com

Oh, the fun never stops when you have plastic to melt – with online shopping you now have even more opportunities to use those credit cards!

Share Globally
http://www.global-investor.com

Have you invested around the world and are unsure how to keep track of your assets? Let Global Investor keep you up-to-date with your portfolio.

Ssh! – It's Unofficial
http://www.angelfire.com/al/bbbugle/

Many unofficial investment tips can be found here – just make sure you don't tell anyone!

Money Street
http://www.thestreet.com

Up-to-date news by leading reviewers
on insurance, stocks and shares. Forums
hold discussions on topics such as 'Going
back to work, is it worth it when you've
got kids?'.

Fake It!
**http://hometown.aol.com/
twelfth1/page/money.htm**

If you want to get rich quick, why not
simply buy a fortune? These tricksters are
selling phoney million dollar bills online.

Millionaire Secrets
http://www.he.net/~brady/secret.html

At this site you will find the tools to
succeed – did you know that self-
employed people are four times more
likely to become millionaires?

Easy Come, Easy Go!
http://www.thanksamillion.com/

Millionaire philanthropist Percy Ross has set up this site to advertize the fact that he once had a million and then…gave it all away!

Hanging on a Limb
http://www.familytreemaker.com/ users/g/e/a/tim-h-geary/

Look up your ancestors at this site that helps you trace your family tree. There may be an inheritance lying around with your name on it!

Mrs Cohen
http://www.mrscohen.com

Mrs Cohen dishes out stock market advice, industry news and a financial quote of the day to give you inspiration, at this money site.

Money Talks
http://www.talks.com/

An online magazine for the serious investor – cheaper than buying the magazine and it talks back too!

Finders Keepers
http://www.foundmoney.com

If you've lost money, go to this site, type in your personal details and they'll put a trace on any foreign accounts that may be in a vault waiting for you to collect it!

Buy, Buy; Sell, Sell
http://quicken.excite.com

An investment page featuring top business news, details of share prices and how the world markets have performed…very Excite-ing!

Microsoft
http://moneycentral.msn.com/investor/
Microsoft's money page must be good
– look what it did for Bill Gates!

Feeling Lucky?
http://www.whitebuffalocasino.com/
If you're feeling lucky, why not try your
hand at the various casino games and
horse racing at this site? Play either for
fun or for real money!

'Millionaire' Magazine
http://www.millionaire.com

If you're having trouble thinking of ways to dispose of all your hard-earned cash, read the profiles of millionaires from the last century and how they spent their millions.

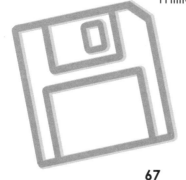

Cry "Yahoooo"!
http://quote.yahoo.com/

You'll be out on the rooftops shouting "Yahoooo" when you discover your shares are riding high at this up-to-date site!

What Do You Get?
http://www.businessfinancemag.com/

Does your salary match your true net worth? To find out, visit this online magazine's site.

Easy Tax
http://listen.to/taxman

It's a real pain to have to work out your tax and there is always the risk you'll get it wrong! However, help is on hand at this site that aims to make tax easy.

Own That Business
http://www.inc.com

Have you a business idea you're bursting to develop? Whatever the idea, before becoming your own boss you should consult this site for practical advice.

Make It Big!
http://www.taps.com

'A change is as good as a rest', so the old saying goes! So visit this site that lists hundreds of jobs up for grabs in Europe. Brush up on your language skills first!

Share Pages
http://www.sharepages.com

Up-to-the-minute share news and rates can be found here, along with a forum for members to exchange and discuss share tips and info.

Get Paid to Surf
http://paid-surf.goldeneyes.com

We all know that from here on in, the only way to make it big is in the Dot.com game. This site offers opportunities to earn while you surf.

Internet Fortunes
http://www.freeyellow.com/ members3/tmo-itd/index.html

If your dream is to become a Dot.com millionaire, your best bet is to read the hot tips found here.

71

FT

http://ftyourmoney.com

The *Financial Times* money page aims to help the reader with everything from home buying to pensions – there's even a 'To Do' list to get you started!

Millionaire's Notebook

http://www.aeu-inc.com/ cgi-local/shop.pl/page

An inspirational book that reassures you that even ordinary Joes can make it big if they want it badly enough!

The Girl Next Door
**http://www.stretcher.com/
stories/970616c.htm**

The only thing better than the girl next door is the millionaire next door, according to this witty book review.

E=MC^{2}

**http://www.smartcalc.com/
cgi-bin/smartcalc/sav1.cgi/tomdean**

There has to be a formula to making it rich! If Einstein figured out relativity, someone can suss out the formula to millionarity! Here are some possibilities…

Dirty Dozen
http://ftc.gov/opa/1998/9807/dozen.htm

Here you can find a list of the 12 most common Internet scams – don't get caught, read them before they happen to you!

News Over the Atlantic
http://www.nyse.com

Find out what's happening to shares in the city that never sleeps.

Listed List
http://www.hemscott.com

Need help tracing a company? Make this site, featuring a huge database of publicly quoted companies, your first stop.

Understand Finance
http://www.ibm.com/financialguide/

IBM's finance page will guide you from getting started through to investor's tips – there's also a handy online glossary of terms to help you wade through the jargon.

Time For Finance
http://www.ft.com

This is a great place to visit for up-to-date business and financial news, and registration is totally free.

US Updates
http://www.amex.com

Check out movements on the Dow Jones, S&P and NASDAQ indexes.

Oz Highs and Lows
http://www.asx.com

If you've invested 'down under', this is the site to visit for share prices, info on upcoming floats, and company announcements.

Hong Kong for a Song
http://www.sehk.com.hk

The Hong Kong Stock Exchange home page, with subtitles for those who need them!

Young Investors
http://www.younginvestor.com/pick.shtml

You're never too young to start thinking about your finances, so log on here to pick from Gnaz Dax, Webster or Blad as your cyber guide to the world of money.

Cor Blimey
http://www.ftse.com/

Whether you're looking to take out an option on a Norwegian stock, or sell a Footsie 100 company, all the pricing information you need is right here.

New York, New York
http://www.nyse.com

Find out what is happening to shares in the city that never sleeps.

Make Friends With Tax!
**http://www.lineone.net/
clubs/money/tax/taxfront-d.html**

Register here to get acquainted with
the taxman for helpful information on
self-assessment, family trusts and capital
gains tax.

The Supplementary Number
http://www.cashwiz.com

OK, stop dreaming, and win loads of money in a flash by entering this free Internet lottery draw.

Which Bank?
http://www.mybank.com

With so many to choose from, this directory of banks on the Net covers the world, but is listed by continent to make searching easy.

World Bank
http://www.worldbank.org

Find out all about a bank dedicated to fighting poverty by raising money for development programs – their goal is a world free of poverty.

Wall Street
http://www.wsj.com

The *Wall St Journal*'s transatlantic news site. Stay one step ahead!

Free Lunch
**http://www.webchurch.org/
scotfree/index.htm**

This site provides a list of online freebies,
including free domain names that may
be worth something later!

Words and Phrases
http://www.investorwords.com

Ever been frustrated by all the financial
terms, buzzwords and phrases that are
continually changing or being added?
This site removes the jargon so you'll
never be confused again!

83

Need Cash?
http://www.homepagenow.com/money.html

Finding it hard to raise the money to start your own webpage? Visit the site that gives you excellent advice on how to seek sponsors.

Ten on the Nose
http://www.bluesq.com

If you're the gambling type that likes to live life on the edge, this site is definitely for you!

What to Do With Cash?
**http://www.umva.com/
~clay/money/index.html**

Make origami animals out of it, of
course! To find more fabulous things to
do with all those spare notes you have
lying around, get online and log on to
this wacky site.

Franchise Anyone?
http://www.lds.co.uk/franchise/

All you need to know about owning and
operating a franchise.

Personal Advisor
http://www.thisismoney.com

A friendly online personal advisor is on hand at this site. Aimed at the average consumer rather than the practised investor, it offers practical day-to-day advice.

Growing Business
http://smallbusiness.yahoo.com

If you have just started your own business and need advice on how to make it blossom, then this is the web site for you.

Motley Fool
http://www.motleyfool.com/

Their aim is to educate, amuse and enrich you at this finance site – enter the 'Fun and Folly' section and you never know what you might find!

Picasso Please
http://www.artrepublic.com

Many people have made a lot of money buying and selling art. This site is worth having a look at to see exactly how.

Le Chalet
http://www.french-property.com

Every le millionaire needs le holiday home in France. Non?

Get the Toolbox
http://www.edgeonline.com

Practical questions and answers to everyday problems experienced by small businesses. It's always good to hear how others have successfully dealt with similar problems!

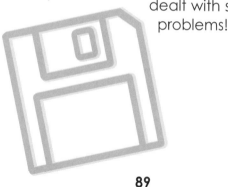

89

Money Mail
http://www.bankone.com/
If you need to send Money Mail urgently
to friends and family, this web site allows
you to do so with the greatest of ease.

Forum on Finance
http://www.inc.com
Discussions are constantly underway
on this US-based web site, which is also
the home of a top-selling finance
magazine.

Fast Lane
http://www.edgeonline.com

An informative online magazine for entrepreneurs who are keen to make their mark on the Net.

Never Too Young
http://www.kidsmoney.org

A useful parental guide which features everything from the top ten financial principles you should impress upon your children, to tips on how kids should do paid chores.

Celeb Payouts
**http://www.forbes.com/
forbes/00/0320/6507161a.htm**

Which star earns $20 million per movie,
and who gets paid $80,000 for a one-
hour speech? See the going rates for
celebs at this mag's site.

Big Boys' Toys
http://yachts.com/sales.html

If money is no object, why not buy the
ultimate big boy's toy at this site – a gin
palace to cruise around the South of
France!

Ex Rates
http://finance.yahoo.com/

Visiting Italy shortly and need to find out how many lira there are to the dollar? It's as simple as pie with this currency converter.

Measuring Measures
http://www.french-property.com/ cgi-bin/ifp/convert.pl

Whether it's lengths, volumes, weights, or temperatures you're looking for, you can convert them all easily here at this informative site.

Give Me a Price
http://ceoexpress.com/

With links to major US newspapers and newsfeeds, as well as a huge database of securities and prices, this site is a must for any serious investor.

Raging Bull
http://www.ragingbull.com

Investment news and breaking headlines can be found at this site that claims to be 'leading the investor revolution'.

Hot Stock!
**http://cbs.marketwatch.com/
news/newsroom.htx**

If you want the story behind the
numbers, this is the web site to visit. It
even boasts a hot stock tracker where
you can keep track of your favorite five
stocks.

Minty Fresh
http://www.usmint.gov/

Take a tour of the US Mint and find out
all there is to know about making
money…literally!

95

3

GADGETS AND
GIZMOS

Dodgy.com
http://www.books4you.addr.com/

Feeling mischievous? Then log on to
this wicked site which will point you in
the direction of a fake celebrity driver's
license or a remote-controlled fart
machine!

Your Mission
http://www.spy.th.com/other.html

Live out your 007 fantasies at this online
'Advanced Intelligence Spy Shop' and
get your hands on small wireless video
cameras and disappearing ink pens.

97

My Alarm
**http://www.homestead.com/
excuse_me/excuse_me.html**

Ever been late to work and the 'public transport' excuse has resulted in the evil eye? No problem! – this gem gives you an excuse and makes you look witty too.

Cool Runnings
http://www.electronicgizmos.com

Imagine being able to start your car and its heater from the warmth of your breakfast table! Imagine no longer, for it is now a reality at this innovative site.

Past Products
http://www.toad.net/
~andrews/bobbypin.html

An entire site dedicated to one man's memory of twentieth-century products, including the bobby pin, cufflinks and watch fobs! A fun step back in time.

Virtual Babe
http://www.ananova.com

It was bound to happen – the world's first virtual newscaster! She's a cyber babe – and she can tell you the latest news too!

What TV?
http://www.parentsoup.com/ parentspicks/soft/tribble.3-12.23_20.html

At this great site you can purchase gadgets for your kids that teach as well as being fun – who needs TV?

Are You Invited?
http://www.invitemetoo.com

Looking for an easy way to organize a party? Then this site will prove invaluable – choose a design, enter email addresses, and 'hey presto', an instant party…just add friends!

100

Yo-Yo
http://www.gadgetsandgizmos.com

Let this site fill you in on all the latest
fads and crazes, and stock up on
everything from lava lamps to talking
picture frames.

Neat!
http://www.neatsite.com/gadgets.htm

A huge selection of useful things to
make life easier at home, while
travelling, fixing the car, or surfing the
Net. Why sweat the small stuff?

Glowing Sock
http://www.nando.com/newsroom/ntn/biz/051498/biz29_21768_noframes.html

They've invented a way to find matching socks in the dark at this site – might be a handy way to find them when only one comes out of the wash also!

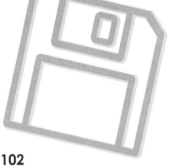

102

Fruit Powered Clocks
http://www.greatgiftsandgadgets.com/ gadgets

You can stop looking as everything you ever wanted is here – glow pens and fruit powered clocks to name a few!

What Do You Think?
http://www.gisentinel.com/ features/technology/forums/gg

Share your ideas on what you feel will be the next 'big thing' here – a great way to suss out a product before you actually buy it.

Buy It
http://www.billionaires.html

Get your wad of cash out and purchase a luxury watercraft or precious gem. Whatever your heart desires, you'll find it at Billionaires Boulevard.

Test Site
http://www.australia.cnet.com/ briefs/comparisons/gizmos/

The people behind this web site have the terrible job of testing all the products that end up on their desks each week – all you have to do is choose the best!

Super Solver
http://www.supersolver.com

See if you can get your head around the challenging brainteasers featured here. Don't worry, it's in a game format and if you love it, you can buy it!

Simon Says
http://www.gadgets.search-mysimon.com/

Need a helping hand with the shopping? Let this online shopper lighten the load by tracking down the best deals and the latest gadgets so you don't have to.

Love Poetry
http://www.emrkt.com/shop_emrkt/

Earn extra points by sticking a poem
on the refrigerator for your partner –
check this web site to purchase a set of
magnetic poetry.

Gadgetronix
http://www.gadgetronix.com

Put your sunglasses on before you enter
this blinding sight – it has all kinds of
both strange and sensible electronic
goods for your home, office and car.

MP3
http://www.wired.com/news/gizmos/

If you have become addicted to the latest music technology to hit the worldwide web, then this site allows you to purchase all your MP3 needs at one place.

Can't Get Enough
http://www.sony-cp.com

Site of one of the leading manufacturers of MP3 units – it doesn't matter how you play it, just play it loud!

On the Go
**http://www.currents.net/magazine/
national/1706/mobo_1706.html**

If you've booked a vacation, but can't
bear to leave your computer at home,
buy the latest goods here to protect it.

American Science
**http://4gadgets.4anything.com/network
-frame/0,1855,3609:12693,00.html**

You can buy everything from shrunken
heads to 'Statue of Liberty' torches at
this weird and wacky site!

Lights, Camera, Action
http://www.barbizon.com/ photocat/gripgadget.html

One for all budding photographers out there – this site will solve all your lighting problems and includes a huge range of adapters, clamps and magic arms.

Mouse Trap
http://www.accumentinc.com/atrap.htm

The only mouse these clever monkeys are trapping is you, by selling clever, innovative goods for the computer and home.

It's Life, Jim
http://www.scifi-uk.com

Trekkie alert – this site was designed for all sci-fi fans. Order trilogy box sets of 'Star Trek' and 'Star Wars' to be sent directly from cyberspace to your door!

No More Bets
http://member.aol.com/
glerp/g/gadgets.html

Pretend you're typing the latest financial report while you're really gambling! – it's all perfectly legal though because no money actually changes hands.

Pay Attention Bond!
**http://www.geocities.com/
timesquare/bunker/6254/gadgets.html**

Too busy dreaming you were 007 to
notice the gadgets in the latest movie?
Well, this site has them all listed for you!

Home Brew
**http://www.21stcenturyplaza.com/
wine/gadget.html**

If you're the type who likes to brew his
own beer, this site will supply home-
brewing goodies such as iceless chillers.

Air Guitar
**http://www.zdnet.com/
pcmag/issues/1422/pcm_00162.htm**

Continually update your computer at
this site – they have a special plug for air
guitar rock stars!

Cheats Beware
**http://www.westward.com/
club/trivia20.htm**

Who used Oxygum and why? Find the
answer to this and other TV gadget trivia
questions at this brain-taxing site.

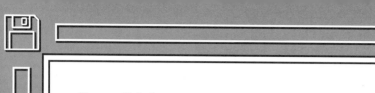

Here It Is!
http://hitechdepot.com/

Been online shopping all day and still can't find that special something? – this web site stocks all kinds of gadgets from Video Color Enhancers to Triple Tray DVD Players.

113

For the Blind
http://ntiserver.blind.state.ia.us/howto/gadgets.htm

Do you have a visually impaired friend?
All the gizmos developed for the non-
seeing are here, including talking clocks
and watches.

Make It Yourself!
http://www.invention.com

If your creative juices are flowing, have
a chat to this online patent attorney.
That remote-controlled lawn mower
could make you a fortune!

Gizmo Mall
http://www.gizmomall.com/

'Your source for Innovative Lifestyle Technology' site includes ultra-light planes to assemble and zappy scooters to keep you amused for hours!

Best Toys Win
http://home.zdnet.com/ anchordesk/story/story_2477.html

Jesse Berst believes that "whoever dies with the best toys wins". Check out his site – the best are all listed here, such as digital books and digital compasses.

PDA Sheet
http://www.pdastreet.com

PDA does not just stand for 'Public Displays of Affection' – at this site you will find the latest in computing goods and gizmos.

Etoys
http://www.etoys.com

Don't let the kids tell you what they want for Christmas – be inspired and shock the socks off them with the cool toys here, such as a Talking Electronic Dartboard.

116

Spam
http://www.spam.com

For lovers of luncheon meat everywhere, purchase anything remotely related to 'Spam' at this site. Great buys include a pair of 'Spam' flip-flops.

Stuck For a Gift?
http://www.stuckforagift.com

Can't think of a gift for that special someone? Help is at hand at this web site where gifts include alien glow-in-the-dark clocks!

117

On the Web!
http://www.gadgetsontheweb.com

From underwater cameras to foldable compasses, this nifty site is definitely gadget heaven.

Play That Funky Music
http://www.creative.com

This site claims to 'let you plug into the power of the Internet to experience digital entertainment beyond your PC', and lets you choose the best audio products around.

Burn Baby Burn!
http://www.guillemot.com

Simply choose your country of origin and this site will present you with the latest in gaming equipment and recording wizardry.

MP3 Please
http://www.thomson-lyra.com

This is the place to come to download the latest MP3s – vote for your favorite or tell a friend!

Choo Choo
http://www.biglittle.com

For the ardent train enthusiast – small-scale train models and other train accessories are all available at the online 'Big Little Railroad Shop'.

Remotely Interested?
http://www.towerhobbies.com

Radio Controlled Models abound at this site – from airplane kits through to race simulators. Check out the beginner's section to get started!

Weird and Wacky!
http://www.online-catalog.com
A site dedicated to everything weird and wacky, including All-Hazard Radios and StreetPilots so you need never ask for directions shamefully again!

Tee-rific
http://www.golf-gadgets.com

This site easily fulfils all your golfing needs – where else could you buy a Thermal Whizz GolfPack Cooler?

My Compliments
http://complimentstothechef.com/index.html

Claiming to be a 'kitchen store and more', this site is 'brimming with the wonderful, incredible, amazing, eclectic, practical...' – or so they claim themselves!

Kitchen Gadgets
http://www.kitchen-classics.com/

Use your chopping board as a mouse pad and get online to buy some cool gadgets for your kitchen, such as crème brulee torches and electric ice shavers.

Make Life Easy
http://www.hometownvariety.com

Life could be so easy if you only owned the Sore Loser Electric Massager or a Telephone Voice Changer. Well, now you know where to get them!

Electronic Gadgets
**http://www.gatewayelex.com/
index2.htm**

Do you want to keep your kids out of
the refrigerator at night? Then log on
here to find useful goodies such as
a Talking Motion
Detector and
a Mini CCD
Camera.

124

On Vacation
http://beachcomber.com/

If you need help carrying all your gadgets down to the beach, log on here for the ultimate in leisure time gadgetry such as a 'Beach Caddy'.

Spies Like Us
http://www.detroitnews.com/ menu/stories/50691.htm

"We don't sell toys" boasts the owner of this spy shop site, so click on to grab the latest pair of serious night-vision goggles or a spy camcorder.

125

Being Watched!
http://www.spooktech.com

An online shopping paradise for all your surveillance needs. Log on to watch 'Busted On The Job III' – a web-cam that catches employees misbehaving!

Hot Toys
http://www.gismo-world.com

A site full of hot toys, from personal robot companions to whale-sounding mouse pads to help ease your day at the office.

Space Age
http://www.smarthome.com

The latest in home automation and security for those dreaming of their own space-age home.

Gifts Galore
http://www.k2man.co.uk

First-class site of branded and hand-crafted quality gifts for men – watches, cufflinks and sexy bathrobes...for that personal touch!

Watch Out!
http://www.wonderfullywacky.com

A site guaranteed to contain the extraordinary – how about a 'Poop Mouse Candy Dispenser'? Just raise his head and stand clear of the rear!

Cutting Edge
http://www.topixonline.com

The undisputed leader of innovation! Check out the cutting edge gifts, from the newest Imac radio to an electric car.

High as a Kite!
http://www.weirdmall.com

Ever wanted to go 'parabouncing' to 100 feet? Well, check this amazing site out to get the low-down.

Brief Encounter
http://www.skivvy.com

This site offers the personal touch when it comes to undies as gifts...a different pack of goodies for every month!

Life on the Edge
http://www.alt-gifts.com

This alternative gift company's web site offers big toys for big boys, and for the adventure freaks amongst us, they even offer life-on-the-edge experiences!

Toys 4 Guys
http://toys4guys.com

You are now entering the world of the latest funky gismos. Feeling peckish? Visit the 'Belly Shop' for all your favorite goodies!

In the Doghouse
http://www.doghouse-gifts.com

If you're in the doghouse, visit this site. Offering gifts for all occasions, they can be personalized to help you out of any tricky situation and back into the good books!

Wacky Shack
http://www.4gadgets4anything.com

This wacky shack site takes you to a wondrous gizmo site – the guru will lead the way to enlighten you on what's hot and what's not!

Seeing is Believing
http://www.greatgiftsandgadgets.com

Stuck for ideas for that special gift? Then check out a site full of unusual goodies such as night-vision goggles!

Tomorrow's World
http://cgi.bbc.co.uk/tw/stories/gadgets

Based on the British TV program, this futuristic site features the advance technologies of tomorrow, such as electric shock car locks and a robotic lawn mower.

132

Gadgets Galore
http://gadgets-galore.modifications.com/

Visit this global gadget site for the latest in 'Playstation' equipment and Internet mobile phones.

Gadget News
http://www.gadgetnews.com/

Read the low-down on all the latest gadget technology at this interesting site, featuring ever-glowing pens and a Quicktionary Instant Translator.

Gadget Ezine
http://www.gadget.co.za

Follow the latest in gadget technology news and read reviews of the latest hi-tech goods, such as wrist communication devices and laptops for kids.

Gadget Boy
http://www.gadgetboy.com/

Reviews with attitude appear in this weekly online gazette, with updates on video and imaging, audio and music, games, and other gizmo goodies.

Gadget Shop
http://thegadgetshop.co.uk/
TGS/defaultframes.asp

A range of weird and wonderful oddities, such as lighter lipsticks and The Truth Machine can be purchased online at very affordable prices.

Street Tech
http://www.streettech.com/

Brush up on your tech terms with the Street Tech glossary featured at this web site, and check the ratings of the latest gizmos such as Inverse Symbolic Calculators.

Just Robots
http://kdorsey.hom.mindspring.com/

Start your very own collection of vintage robots at this site dedicated entirely to robots – check out the gallery of cyber rogues.

136

The Gizmo Page
http://www.courier-journal.com/gizweb/index.html

This special ezine page from this online newspaper features the best in new gadgets and gizmos, such as silent instruments and the latest computers.

Tech Museum
http://store.thetech.org/scientecgiff.html

Stylish technology toys for grown-ups are available at the Tech Museum Online Store, such as tabletop holographic displays and anti-gravity Levitron Tops.

137

Cool Tools
http://www.cooltool.com/

This web site brings you the coolest tools on the Web and hardware that goes beyond the hype.

Firebox
http://www.firebox.com/gadgets/index.html

If remote-controlled UFOs, projection clocks and voice mail postcards are your idea of fun, check out this web site which claims that it is 'where men buy stuff'!

Fantasy T-Shirts
http://www.smallfaces.com

This creative T-shirt company had the neat idea of T-shirts decorated with the torso of a fantasy character and you provide the 'head'. There are over 30 great designs to choose from.

Goofy Inventions
http://www.totallyabsurd.com

Award-winning site that investigates funny inventions – there are hundreds of time-wasting treasures here, such as the kissing shield and the giant duck decoy!

Living Gadget
http://www.jfkhealthworld.com/ LivingGad/livgad.htm

Can you guess what the most incredibly complex gadget in the world could be? Take a dive in here to find out.

Acme Widgets
http://www.inil.com

Gadget games for those who should really be working! Use your keyboard to play speedracer in a Grand Prix, or pretend your cursor is a set of hot wheels as you speed around a track!

Gadget Whiz
http://www.newscientist.com/ lastword/gadgets.html

Put the experts at this site on the hot spot by posting your thorniest gadget questions on their message board, and while you wait for an answer, search the archive.

Gizmo Mania
http://www.gadgets-inc.com/

Recorders, telephones, scanners, surveillance equipment and other snooping stuff are all available here!

4

ENTERTAINMENT

Twentieth Century Fox
http://www.foxmovies.com

Check out the latest clips, trailers, and gossip on upcoming Hollywood blockbuster movies. Just don't expect the reviews to be entirely objective!

Books, Books, Books
http://www.amazon.com

This site has one of the world's largest selection of books for you to browse through and buy. If you fancy reviewing the latest release, you are welcome to put your thoughts online.

Brit Flicks
http://www.filmfour.com

Remember 'Trainspotting'? Check out the Film Four web site – a company that produces anything but costume dramas!

Disney Heaven
http://www.disney.com

For kids and grown-ups alike, this colorful and impressive site will give you previews of their forthcoming movies. Fun for all ages.

144

Miramax
http://www.miramax.com

Find out where to see the next Greenaway or Brunel films at this site dedicated to hip movies and their directors.

I'd Like to Thank...
http://www.oscars.org

Get your tuxedo out for a red-carpet visit to the site dedicated to Hollywood glamor and talent. Yes, it's the official site for Oscar.

Six Degrees
http://www.astrophile.com

A fascinating site that searches for
connections between actors and
actresses, and the films they have
starred in. Hollywood is far smaller than
you would imagine!

146

Reel Classics
http://www.reelclassics.com

A brilliant site all about the movie greats! Wallow in nostalgia – they don't make 'em like they used to!

Trappings of Fame
http://www.yack.com

This site features interviews with celebs about the fame game – both the advantages and disadvantages (if there are any!).

Movie Bible
http://www.uk.imdb.com

Claiming to be 'the biggest, best, most award-winning movie site on the planet', you can check out the photos and trailers of forthcoming blockbusters, and read celeb news and interviews here.

Ain't it Cool?
http://www.aint-it-cool-news.com

A well-informed Hollywood insider spills all the gossip and news for you to enjoy – find out who's currently considered hot and who's not!

Mr Showbiz
http://www.mrshowbiz.go.com

You've heard of the virtual newscaster...now meet the virtual film reporter! Mr Showbiz will give you all the info you need on the latest Tinsel Town news and views.

149

The Beeb
http://www.beeb.com

Chat, gossip, and reviews on all your favorite British TV shows can be found at the site of one of the world's most well-renowned television channels.

Virtual Cinema
http://www.afionline.org

Sit in front of your computer with a bag of popcorn, and enjoy classic Hollywood films – just make sure the boss doesn't catch you too often!

'Friends'
**http://www.geocities.com/
televisioncity/4151/index.html**

One of Generation X's favorite sitcoms
has it's own web site for you to log onto
and visit the stars of the show. Find out
everything about your favorite TV friends
here.

Movie Making Magic
http://www.film.com

Log on to catch a glimpse of how your
favorite film was made, and to read
interviews with top directors and actors.

151

Monster Review
http://www.cinema.pgh.pa.us/movie/reviews/

If you want the low-down on a film before you pay to see it, check this informative site first which contains a huge database of hundreds of films.

No Good
http://www.movieguru.com

Put your money where your mouth is at this web site, and write your own reviews about the latest movie offerings – then sit back and wait for feedback.

Beatbox Betty
http://www.beatboxbetty.com
Not wanting to be outdone by virtual
film reporter, Mr Showbiz, Beatbox Betty
also provides funky and upbeat
Hollywood reviews from virtual reality
land.

Scripts Ahoy!
http://www.script-o-rama.com
At this web site, you get the chance to
read scripts that have been rejected
and those that, frankly, should have
been!

153

Ultimate Movies
http://www.ultimatemovies.com

Featuring movie news and celebrity headlines, this site will let you know what movies are showing a mere five minutes away from where you live!

Salon Review
http://www.salon.com

A general site that contains a wide range of fun, including books, arts, entertainment, comics and celebrity. If it's not here, it's not happening!

Made Earlier
http://www.badmovies.org

Packed with some of the worst movies ever made, this web site has great info and plot descriptions of films such as 'Cannibal Women in the Avocado Jungle of Death' and 'The Brain from Planet Arous'!

Oh the Humanity!
http://www.ohthehumanity.com

Check out this hilarious site for some
truly toe-curling celluloid catastrophes,
and view 'the worst films ever witnessed
by mortal eyes'. They said it!

Gamespy
http://www.gamespy.com

I spy with my little eye…a program that
is extremely useful for locating games
and servers on the Net. This site also
features a Hall of Fame and the latest
reviews.

Dreamcast
http://www.dreamcast.com

The latest info on Sega's dream machine, plus great links to other gamester sites as well.

Games Arcade
http://www.thearcade.com

Remember when you saved your pennies to go down to the local arcade? Not anymore – log on here for six rooms filled with action-packed games and adventure for free!

Raider Babe
http://www.cubeit.com/ctimes/

Are you hooked on 'Tomb Raider'?
Do you admire the butt-kicking, high
octane goddess that is Lara Croft?
There's lots of great info on this classic
game to be found here.

Cards Bonanza
http://www.zone.msn.com

This mammoth games site brings you
classic card games, such as 'Gin
Rummy' and 'Poker', as well as the best
in virtual reality 3D ones.

158

Where It's At
http://www.ubl.com

You have a song going round your head, you know the band's name but don't know where to find details about them. Log on to this great site and they will give you everything you need to know, apart from their home address of course!

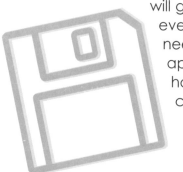

159

Shockwave
http://www.shockwave.com

This multi-media site has an impressive array of choices – log on to games both old and new, cartoons, and greetings. This site really does have it all!

Blaster
http://www.planetunreal.com

Virtual gun-slinging matches have risen in popularity over the last five years, so let off some steam at the end of a hard day by pretending you're John Wayne!

Quake 2000
http://www.quake2000.net/

An edgy and precise online game that will give you sore wrists for days afterwards – the future has arrived!

Mega Games
http://www.gamepost.com

Check out the very latest games at this
fun-packed site, and learn how to play
doubles with someone based on the
other side of the world!

Daddy Frag
http://www.fragdaddy.com

The father of all online 3D games! This
site has info on the game's background
and tips on how to shoot more
accurately.

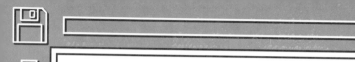

New Releases
http://www.gaming-age.com
Jam-packed with all the latest game
releases, it's time to get with the
program and visit this site that also
features news articles, charts, and
previews.

163

SiN Post
http://www.sinpost.com

Featuring a 'shot of the day', downloads, and regular forums, this games site has something for all fans of the game 'SiN'.

Blizzard
http://www.blizzard.com

Set in the not-too-distant future, 'Blizzard' (for both PC and Mac users) will increase your everyday skills of lying and cheating. Much cheaper than going to law school!

All Music
http://www.allmusic.com
Every trivia-based question on rock, pop, jazz and blues can be found at this huge reference library of a site. Wander the corridors of music for hours.

Bingo
http://www.bingozone.com
You may mock, but this game is curiously addictive and, contrary to popular belief, it isn't just for old ladies! Learn your 'Two Fat Ladies' from your 'Legs Eleven'!

165

100 on Black
http://www.bjrnet.com

Have you always longed to learn how to play 'Blackjack'? Put your money firmly back into your pocket for the moment and get free lessons online.

Games Paradise
http://www.gamesparadise.com

The place to go when you want to buy up-to-the-minute games (in PAL format only), such as 'Daikatana' and 'Cricket 2000' at greatly reduced prices!

166

Game Info
http://www.gamesfaqs.com

Full of features and a tone of arcade games to play online, such as 'Hydro Thunder' and 'Plasma Sword', this site will keep you amused for hours.

News Just In
http://www.ign.com

With an online link to a site where you can rent games, this web site is an entertainment bonanza of sci-fi comics, new game releases, and even a movie section.

Action Man
http://www.actionman.com

A great visual site featuring an online game starring that favorite childhood friend, Action Man.

Game Week
http://gameweek.com

If you want to become seriously involved in the games industry, this online magazine has all the headlines, events and industry news, plus a featured jobs section.

168

Cheat Site
http://www.xcheater.com

Can't quite make it to the last level?
Let this online cheat site give you a few
pointers in the right direction.

Dungeons and Dragons
http://www.geocities.com/area51/8306/

'Dungeons and Dragons' is just as
popular now as it has ever been.
Rediscover this classic game or log on
here to have a go if you missed it the
first-time round.

169

Hotting Up
http://www.heat.net/

This Sega site will allow you to use its great range of online arcade games for free, but if you want to use the bigger, more advanced games, you'll have to subscribe. However, it does pay you to play!

170

Games and Videos
http://www.gamesandvideos.com

Thousands of games and thousands of videos on sale at one enormous site. It does take a while to download, but if you pre-order new games, you will also save money.

Online Competition
http://www.toasted.com

Download this free trivia quiz and compete against other online players. You'll discover that "you're not as smart as you like to think you are".

Doomsday
http://www.doomnation.com

'Doom' is back – stronger and deadlier than ever before! Have a rematch with an old friend and see if they can beat you at 'Deathmatch' too!

Freebie Games
http://www.gameszone.com

This web site covers all games within Europe, so dust down your console and have a great day indoors!

172

Addicts
http://www.gameaddict.net

Before you check yourself into GAA
(Games Addict Anonymous), visit this
site – it features all the reviews and
latest demos of PC games. You won't
be able to resist!

Cheaterama
http://www.cheatstation.com

If you're going nuts, here's a great site
that lets you pick its brain to solve that
gaming dilemma – it claims to provide
16,962 codes for 6,096 games!

Party On!
http://www.ministryofsound.com

The cool site of one of the world's hottest dance clubs – hear all the latest mixes by their top resident DJs.

Jungle Boogie
http://www.jungle.com

Looking for an all-in-one shop that stocks your entire entertainment needs? 'Jungle' is a warehouse on the Web with tons of top-brand computers, software, videos and games.

174

Top 100
http://www.cddb.com

Who really hit the top of the charts this week? This site calculates the number of hits each band has had, and then compiles the hit list from the entire Internet-using populace.

Music Man
http://www.peoplesound.com

If you tell the guys at this site the type of music you enjoy, they will compile a personal list of tracks for you to download and listen to!

MP3
http://www.mp3.com

Confused about the latest technology in music? This site explains MP3s in clear and concise terms so you won't feel ignorant and left out.

Get Down
http://www.mp3now.com

Once you've sorted out your MP3 knowledge, it's time to start using it. This is one of the most popular MP3 portals on the Net. Log on and listen!

MP3 Search
http://www.mp3.lycos.com

Start your search for all things MP3-related here. Be warned – once you start, you won't be able to stop as there are some amazing link sites featured here too.

Wanna Record Contract?
http://www.musicunsigned.com

This site features music by bands who don't as yet have a record contract – vote for your favorite. It also features music news, info and festival dates.

177

Time Out
http://www.timeout.com

A comprehensive online guide to gigs and clubs featuring all types of music worldwide can be found here at this cool ezine site.

Audio Dynamite
http://www.audiostreet.com

Got a scratch on your favorite record, but haven't got round to buying the CD version yet? Visit this site for a vast collection of CDs and an excellent back catalog.

MTV
http://www.mtv.com

The most famous music television station now has its own web site, featuring exclusive interviews with top artists and movie soundtrack downloads.

Addicted to Noise
http://www.addict.com

Jam-packed news and reviews site, with a heavy bias toward the rock end of the music spectrum.

179

Strike a Pose
http://www.wbr.com/madonna/

If the 'material girl' makes you want to
strike a pose, check out her very own
web site. It's packed with the latest
sizzling news and gossip on the ever-
changing Ms Ciccone.

The Stones
http://www.the-rolling-stones.com

They keep on rolling and gather no
moss, so visit the baddest boys in rock
and find out what they are up to at the
moment – they're still misbehaving!

Bowling

**http://directory.netscape.com/
Arts/Music/Music_That_Sucks/**

If country music isn't your scene, you'll love this site dedicated to pouring scalding bile over the songs! Check out the song titles, such as 'Velcro Arms, Teflon Heart' and 'I Don't Know Whether to Kill Myself or Go Bowling'!

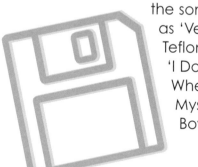

181

Beatlemania
http://www.hollywoodanddivine.com/anthology/index.html

This site features the history and a great photo library of one of the greatest bands of the 60s (some would say of all-time!).

Hotel Trauma
http://www.harmony-central.com

A site written by band members – everything you need to know about performing and acting like a rock star. No TVs out of hotel windows please!

Going for a Song
http://www.sheetmusicdirect.com

Experiencing songwriter's block? – then let this great site provide sheet music for you to download at those times when the harmony just won't happen!

365 Music
http://www.music365.com

Here's a site full of daily album reviews, flashbacks, and interviews on the best concerts. You can also purchase heavily-discounted CDs, videos, and digital equipment.

183

Bite-Sized Reviews
http://www.foocha.com

A fresh new site that features 40 resident,
individual and honest writers, reviewing
everything in the world of entertainment.
Log on for the very latest!

Video Hits and Misses
http://www.vh1.com

This music channel is now available in
cyberspace and showcases artists that
have now disappeared from stardom –
revisit the bad hair and clothes of your
youth!

Trivia Heaven
http://www.80's.com/who_normal.htm

Great resource for parties – simply print off the 80s trivia questions at this site and let the fun begin!

Music Madness
http://www.allstarmag.com

If you click on here, you will be fed reviews on the very latest music releases, from Cliff Richard to Bon Jovi.

All Singing, All Dancing
http://www.musicals101.com

From 'Singin' in the Rain' to 'Les Miserables', this web site is packed with news and info on the shows that have been pulling people into the theaters for years.

Blues Baby
http://www.bestblues.com

Put on your shades, grab a shot of bourbon, and tune in here for the listings and reviews of magical blues music.

Country Music
http://www.soundmarket.net/

Come to this site to visit the spiritual home of Dolly Parton, the Dixie Chicks, and Garth Brooks. If it's country, it's here!

Play It Loud
http://www.liveconcerts.com

Did you miss out on tickets for your favorite band's recent concert? Don't despair! – chances are the concert will be replayed at this live online site soon.

5

DREAM
MACHINES

Rolling in Class
http://www.rrab.com/

Rolls Royce and Bentley are synonymous with classy, luxurious cars. This site has photos and a brief history of every model ever built. Timeless classics!

Hog Heaven
http://www.hd-stamford.com

The ultimate two-wheeled machines are shown here in all their glory! Discover that not all Harley-Davidson riders need a forest of facial hair – just most of them!

Water Laughs
http://www.formulaboats.com

We'd all spend our lottery winnings on a
speedboat or three, and this site shows
you just what you could spend your
money on, and how fast it would go!

Wheely Sexy
http://www.fantasycars.com/index.html

Ferrari, Lamborghini, Lotus, Porsche –
all names synonymous with speed,
power, and desire! These machines are
featured in-depth at this site, with envy-
inspiring photos.

Jeepers!
**http://www.corpcomm.net/
~vigenc/mainl.html**

Cory (surname unknown!) has a passion
for Jeeps. Check out his photos of every
type of Jeep imaginable.

Plane Crazy
**http://home.iae.nl/users/
wbergmns/jets.htm**

Budding Top Guns will love this look at
the latest jet fighters. Great action shots
and technical data can be found here,
but not how much they cost!

Strip Tease
http://www.dragracingunderground.com

The ultimate fantasy cars are shown in fantastic tyre-burning action at this site. Great photos and videos give an insight into those lucky enough to be allowed behind the wheel!

Boys Toys
http://www.flightfantasy.com

Anyone with a spare $1,000,000 should check out this site for jets, helicopters and yachts that look larger and more luxurious than most homes!

Driven to Distraction
http://www.supercars.net/

Dream machines galore can be found here, with hundreds of photos of the world's most exciting cars. Something for everyone to enjoy – technical info and plenty of shiny metal!

Brawn Lucky
http://www.inlink.com/~iwinkler/

Muscle cars have more grunt than your average run-around. See what makes them so fast, sleek and desirable at this speedy web site.

193

One Small Step
http://www.nssdc.gsfc.nasa.gov/
photo_gallery/photogallery-
spacecraft.html

How many of you dreamt of being an
astronaut when you grew up? Check
out the spacecraft
you could have
flown at this
extraordinary
online photo
gallery!

194

Rotor Way to Go
http://www.members.xoom.com/helicopters/index.htm

A must for whirlybird fans! The latest helicopters in a multitude of exciting action shots. Who needs 'Air Wolf'!

Bug Me
http://www.dune-buggy.com/

Be inspired to fly over sand dunes with only a roll cage between you and the sand at this site. Speed, danger, and big tyres – who could possibly ask for more?

Kitted Out
http://www.angelfire.com/mt/Murena

Kit cars are becoming faster, cheaper and better-looking. Be inspired to dig out your tools at this site, and get down to construction.

Chute Me
http://www.para-cycle.com/

You too can fly through the air on a bike attached to a parachute! This amazing machine is growing in popularity, so check out this web site to view the very latest.

196

Ton of Ship
http://www.warship1.com/default.htm

Explore the world's coolest crafts on and beneath the sea. This site includes features on warships, submarines and aircraft carriers, with great photos and some historical background.

Purr-fect
http://www.jaguarcars.com/

Fast, sleek, shiny…and that's just the web site! Images of every Jag ever made are available here – check out one of the world's most stylish cars in all its glory!

197

Seeing Red
http://www.lau168freeserve.co.uk

Enzo Ferrari's legacy to the world is at
this well-designed web site. Road and
racing models are covered in equal
depth and with equal passion.

Torque of the Town
http://www.njsoper.co.uk

Like your cars to have the highest
possible performance? So does this
site's author – plenty of Maseratis,
Lamborghinis, and McLaren supercars to
keep you happy!

Keep on Truckin'
http://www.layover.com

Not exactly a dream machine, but a great vehicle web site nonetheless, featuring everything to do with the world of trucking!

Lotus
http://www.lotuscars.co.uk

Featuring the latest news and a detailed dealer's guide, this official Lotus web site features a production timeline and, of course, all the info on the cars themselves.

199

Babes
http://come.to/F1Babes
Welcome to the Formula One Babes
picture gallery (any excuse!), and check
out the gorgeous girls who grace the
Formula One scene.

License Plate Mania
http://danshiki.oit.gatech.edu/~iadt3mk/
If the price is right, you can purchase
license plates from anywhere in the
world at this site – from Abu Dhabi to
Western Samoa, take your pick!

Ferrari
http://www.ferrari.it

Italian chic and style are very much in evidence at this bilingual site of one of the ultimate dream machines – check out its history, the cars and upcoming events.

Street Bike
http://www.streetbike.com

Here you will find reviews, gear evaluations, comparisons, and free classifieds, for every type of bike currently available.

Bike Net
http://www.bikenet.com

Place your bids at the online auction
for everything from helmets to bikes
themselves! This site also features
reviews of the latest products and road
test advice.

Paeony F1
http://www.paeony.games.com

You don't have to have the driving skills
of Ralph Schumacher to be allowed on
a Formula One track – this virtual racing
game lets you race safely.

Wheelie Dangerous
http://www.wheelie.com

Watch the Swedish Stunt and Wheel Team perform hair-raising motorcycle stunts at this death-defying site. Check out the Two-Up-Skiing!

It's All Here!
http://www.moto-directory.com

Featuring complete listings of motoring clubs and associations, a great collector's section, and much more, this web site is a motoring paradise.

Crash, Bang, Wallop
http://come.to/F1_crashes

Some are spectacular and some are terrifying! – log on to view some great photo footage of crashes that have occurred in the wonderful world of Formula One.

Porsche
http://www.porsche.co.uk

A name synonymous with glamor and speed – view all the models both old and new, check upcoming events, and find out where you can purchase yours.

204

Top Gear
http://www.topgear.beeb.com

Owners of all makes of vehicles chat online here about their cars, and it is an easy way to find out if a car will suit you. The web site of a popular English motoring TV program, it also features a whole host of road tests and opinions to get you racing.

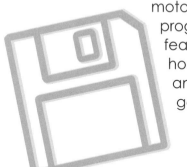

Glamor and Glitz!
http://www.ytmag.com

Parts, supplies, antiques, and restoration advice, can all be found at a site dedicated to this classic piece of machinery! To what am I referring? Log on to find out.

Suzuki Cycles
http://www.suzukicycles.com

Featuring news and interviews, get the low-down on Suzuki's history and enter an online sweepstake to win bikes at this official site.

Aviation Antics
http://www.aso.com

If money is no object, visit the 'Aircraft Shopper Online' site and buy everything from Amphibian planes to an Executive Boeing 737 for $38,000,000!

Aprilia
http://www.aprilia.com

Claiming to be 'the site of wonder', Aprilia's official web site contains up-to-date racing history, and a complete listing of new and old models.

Hot Wheel Auction
http://www.cacars.com

This web site is an auction and
marketing site for all makes and models
of cars, and features great color pics to
ease your fears about purchasing online.

I Want Wheels
http://www.carseverything.com

Whatever your driving requirements, you
are certain to find it here. They can sell
you car parts, send out appraisal forms,
organize free credit, and even let you in
on a few tricks of the trade.

Model Cars
http://www.ewacars.com

If you are a model car enthusiast, visit this site that has one of the largest selections of model cars on the Net.

Antique Machines!
http://www.geocities.com/ motorcity/downs/html

Cars of distinction with side stepping boards! They were the pride of the 1950s – if you missed out, stroll down memory lane for a peek.

209

Easy Rent
http://www.bnm.com/

This user-friendly site lists over 100 rent-a-car agencies worldwide, all located near central airports. Book online and save yourself lots of hassle!

Online Traders
http://www.tradeonline.com

Would you buy a used car from this web site? Make an online offer and you could soon be driving the machine of your dreams.

World of Classic Cars
http://www.classiccarsworld.com

If you enjoy restoring old greats back to glory, you'll love this site. Everything you need to know about purchasing, restoring and maintaining classic cars.

Bumper News!
http://www.carstreet.com

A bumper-to-bumper news and reviews site for all your motoring and biking needs. It also has an informative section called 'Wallet Watch', to help keep your spending under control!

Buick
http://www.buick-parts.com/carsbb.html

Great site for all Buick owners! Find the missing part you've been searching for, or discuss maintenance hiccups with your fellow Buick buddies.

Mr Sport
http://www.mrsport.com

A popular site for avid model car collectors – here you'll find perfect replicas of the adult versions!

212

Slot Cars
http://www.ncphobbies.com

If the only way you are going to be able to race a Formula One car is via the slot car track, then you'll be able to buy your slot cars here. Grown-ups only need apply!

Motors on the Cheap
http://www.carscost.com

Free vehicle specs and a car-buying service that offers cars at dealer prices! What more could you want from an online car yard?

Car Heaven
http://www.cars-on-line.com/

This site is pure classic car heaven! All advertized classic cars on this site are shown with detailed info, so you will be able to purchase with confidence.

Car TV
http://www.carstv.com

No more pushy car salesmen pressuring you for a decision! Here you can shop for second-hand cars in peace, without leaving the comfort of your favorite chair!

214

Planet Motor
http://www.carsmodelcargallery.com/

An excellent model car site with hundreds of model cars on offer, arranged in over 30 categories to make your first choice easy to find.

Motional Memories
http://www.motionalmemories.com

If it's the image of classic cars that sets your blood racing, this web site will take it to boiling point! Superb photos of super cars and vintage vehicles can be found right here!

Sidecars
http://www.ural.com/

The guys at this site import and distribute Russian Ural-style 1930s sidecar motorcycles worldwide – complete the online quiz to see if you deserve to become an owner of one of these classics.

Vintage Etiquette
http://www.historiconline.com/

Learn the secrets of a bygone era by logging on and learning about vintage racing etiquette – comb your sideburns and don't forget your driving gloves!

Auto Hit
http://www.autohit.com

Educate yourself before you purchase your next car! This site outlines info on insurance and how to get a quote – it can even help you track down numberplates.

Yahoo Cars
http://cars.uk.yahoo.com/

Before setting off to purchase your new car, check this online registry first. It lists all cars (both new and old) by make and model, and also has a research column.

Major or Minor
http://www.morrisminors.com

If you love vintage Morris Minors, here's a good place to discuss your passion! Don't delay – join the owner's club today!

The Door Fell Off!
http://www.carsurvey.org

A hilarious site full of disgruntled car owners detailing their motor problems. It's a good idea to log on here before spending your money to get the low-down on specific makes first!

Cash or Charge?
http://www.autohit.com

This sensible site features an 'affordability calculator', which will let you truthfully work out the type of car you can actually afford. Ferrari or Ford?

Car City
http://www.carcity.com

Become a member at this site and they will provide a free 'reminder' service – you'll never forget to change the oil again!

Classic Directory
http://www.classic-car-directory.com

This hot wheel site has a search engine that links all the key components you need to purchase a classic car. Enter a search for the make you want and it will send dealer info back shortly after.

220

Older the Better
http://www.classicar.com

For car enthusiasts, classic motors are often the most valuable and sought after. This site details listings of classic cars for sale, how to revamp those old motors, and includes a spare parts directory.

Online Manuals
http://www.carnet-online.co.uk/haynes/

Forever losing manuals for your vehicle? There are literally hundreds of manuals here for a whole range of different makes and models.

F1 Live
http://www.f1-live.com

For all the Formula One action as it occurs, log on to this exhilarating site. It is overflowing with circuit information, vital statistics and facts about the daredevil drivers.

Bikenet
http://www.bikenet.com

An excellent online bike magazine site that is broken up into different sections for easy searching – it also includes rider talk and bike tests.

The Wheel Thing
http://www.sandsmachine.com

Buy a fold-up travel bike at this unusual site and never worry about public transport or parking spaces ever again! It may also help to keep you fit and trim!

Go!
http://www.formula1.com

There's some great information about the Formula One teams at this site, and also some slick links on who the drivers are and who is currently in pole position.

Cool Bikes
http://www.aboutbikes.com

This site has it all! – information on the sport of cycling, new routes on biking trails, rental news and maintenance tips. A complete bikefest.

Environmental Issue
http://www.zapbikes.com

If it contains gas or diesel, this site won't sell it! But these guys do sell fantastic electric bikes, zappy scooters, and other modes of zero air pollution transport.

All About Cycles
http://www.allaboutcycles.com

Have a search through this web page before your settle on your next motorcycle purchase. There are thousands of used and new motorcycles for sale, as well as links to other cool cycle sites.

Mega Bike
http://www.giant-bicycle.com

For all the latest racing news and the hottest bike information, log on to this giant of a site!

225

Big Dog Bikes
http://www.bigdogmotorcycles.com/

'Big Dog' are the makers of distinctive American motorcycles – they make them to measure and no request is deemed too outlandish!

Harley Burly
http://www.legendmcs.com

If you don't want to part with your beloved Harley but it is in desperate need of parts, log on to this legendary motorcycle parts shop and keep your pride and joy up-to-scratch.

226

Ducati
http://www.ducati.com

Bid online at this Ducati Motor web site for memorabilia, or cruise through their virtual store that features bikes, clothing and accessories. They also want to hear

from you if you would like to open a Ducati store in your town!

227

Red Hot Honda
http://www.hondamotorcycles.com

This is the official Honda motorcycle web site, and it will give you the low-down on Honda's latest designs, specs and features. Plus there are details of their apprenticeship course!

101 For Sale
http://www.100motorcycles.com

Have your classified ad posted onto this web page, and it will automatically be sent to 100 others! Great place to look for a bike to purchase too!

On Yer Bike
http://www.motorcyclesintl.com

Cruisers, touring bikes and sport-touring bikes are all available at this site, so make an offer and apply to join the Hell's Angels as quickly as you can!

Yo Yamaha!
http://www.yamahausa.com/ mc/motorcyc.html

If you've never ridden a Harley, you've never lived! Check out the official site, dedicated to the ultimate bike.

229

Kawasaki
http://www.kawasaki.com

View specs and photos of the bikes they produce, and read all the upcoming race information.

Biker Gang
http://www.conservativebookstore.com/motorcycles/motorcycles.html

All motorcycle riders need a gang, so log on to this excellent site – bikers from all over the world can post their thoughts and opinions, and belong to a virtual gang too!

Motor World
http://www.motorworld.com

Imagine the leader of that biker gang
you see cruising around! Now picture this
online magazine in the same light! –
hugely popular and packs a mean
punch!

Queasy Rider
http://www.insurance-motorcycles.com/

You've got the bike you always dreamed
of – how sick you would feel if your
uninsured bike were stolen! Check out
this site for motorcycle insurance advice.

Auto Ezine
http://www.automotivecatalogs.com/

Claiming to be 'the ultimate source for every automotive enthusiast', this site features parts and accessories for Cameras right through to T-Birds!

Flaming Pig
http://www.fpcycle.com/

A huge range of Japanese and Harley-Davidson bike parts and accessories can be found at discounted prices here – including carburettors, handlebars, engines, and seats.

Hot Metal Mag
http://www.motorcycle.com

An online motorcycle magazine that features a monthly newsletter, a useful chat room, and practical road tests to make you king of the road.

Online Test
http://www.cyberdrive.co.uk

If you are about to take the British driving test, why not do it in cyberspace first to make sure you are up to speed. You can do it time and time again if you need to!

6

SPORT

Laptop Scores
http://www.sportsfeed.com/news

Missed another game because your girl-
friend wanted to watch 'Friends'? Have
your laptop close at hand and log on
here to read the scores as they come in.

Know It All!
**http://www.infoplease.lycos.com/
sports.html**

The world's biggest and most informative
sports reference site, featuring tons of
information and gossip on all sport
around the globe.

235

Ultimate Hero
http://espn.go.com/sportscentury

Cool and comprehensive site dedicated to the sporting heroes of this century – find out who was the ultimate champion in each of your favorite sports.

To the Wall
http://www.allwall.com/asp/

Vast megastore of sports posters for wannabe quarterbacks. Have your favorite sports star sending out winning vibes from your bedroom wall!

Mini *Sports Illustrated*
http://www.sikids.com/index.html

All the info that the grown-up magazine contains (except for the babes in bikinis!), plus the added bonus of a computer games section.

Team Player
http://www.infobeat.com

Simply register your email address and Infobeat will inundate you with up-to-date info, such as scores and news on your favorite team.

237

They Think It's All Over
http://www.soccerage.com

Fantastic video clips of some of the
most famous goals in soccer. This site is
enormous and features listings of teams
worldwide.

Planet Rugby
http://www.planet.rugby.com

As the name suggests, this site is
a winner in terms of worldwide rugby
results, statistics and players, so get
down and dirty with your team.

NFL
http://www.nfl.com

This is the official site of the National Football League, and it features a lot more than the non-official sites. Catch up on the locker room gossip and check out the scores!

Worldwide Sports
http://www.ics.mit.edu/cgi-bin/sports

Seriously cool A–Z of every sport – whatever country you're in, whatever sport you're into, this site is guaranteed to quench your sporting thirst.

Busting Out
http://www.worldortho.com/sportsmed.html

Ever wondered what Miss Universe 1999 looked like? Before you go racing to your computer to take a peek, I'd better explain that this site is dedicated to the bodybuilding Miss Universe!

Hockey Heaven
http://www.playitagainsports.com/

Whether you need a hockey stick or a puck, click on to this site for all your hockey needs, plus an indepth look at this fast and furious game.

Home Run
http://www.geocities.com/~andrea

Site made by the fans, for the fans, on one of the world's best-loved sports...baseball! This site includes a full index of the best players around.

Speed!
http://sports.yahoo.com/rac/nascar

Strap on your seatbelt, adjust your helmet, and hold on tight! – this fantastic Daytona site is bang up-to-date with the latest, exhilarating racecar action.

Swedish Games
http://www.kfk.org/

Join Sven and his friends as they battle the rest of the world for international Frisbee titles.

242

Cyber Workout
http://www.turnstep.com

No puffing and panting in an aerobics class any longer, because the future is cyber aerobics! Top instructors shriek encouragement to you all on one well-toned site!

Real Tennis
http://www.real-tennis.com

'Real Tennis' started in Elizabethan England and was known as the 'Game of Kings'. Wimbledon tennis has derived from it, so log on and check it out.

Table Tennis-tastic!
http://www.ittf.com

This site is a must for all fans of this amazingly fast-paced table game. It's packed with information, a chat room, and tips on how to beat the opponent!

Triathlon
http://www.triathletemag.com

Training schedules, diet tips and everything else in between can be found at this ezine site for greedy people not content with only doing one sport at a time!

244

Dirtragmag
http://www.dirtragmag.com

Much more than the Tour de France, this terrific mountain bike ezine is packed to the brim with reviews, health and fitness news, as well as an interactive opinion page.

Get the Rush!
http://www.aerial.org/

Are you an adrenaline junkie? Then this site should give you a great fix of hair-raising action! You name it, these guys can organize for you to do it!

Ski Central
http://www.skicentral.com/

Track down all the info you require to organize your winter sports program here. This site connects to over 5,500 snow sport sites and features ski reports and snow-cams.

Betting Bonanza
http://www.sporting-life.com

If you're thinking of placing a bet on an upcoming sport's event, check here for the insider tips first. Then check if you can afford to lose next week's rent money!

Hang Ten
**http://www.watertrader.com/
magazine/surfing-guide.htm**

Get away from your computer, slip into
a wetsuit, and clear your mind. How? By
surfing, of course! Read the low-down
here before you hit the waves.

Kicking Karate
http://www.blackbeltsearch.com

A massive directory full of martial arts sites worldwide. Here's where you learn the ultimate in focus, stamina and concentration.

Legends
http://www.cmgww.com/sports.html

Want to know more info about the life of Mohammad Ali, or perhaps it's Michael Jordan that you idolize. For fans both young and old, your legends are all waiting here!

White Men Can't Jump
http://www.netguide.com/ guide/sports/nba.htm

Who says? This cool site brings you up-to-date information and gossip on all your basketball favorites.

Golf Buggy
http://www.golfmajors.com

Sit in your golf buggy and take in all the swinging action! All the results and play of the US Open, the PGA, the Masters, and the British Open, can be viewed here.

Sheer Height
http://www.bouldering.com/

For lovers of risk and the great outdoors, this is the site for climbers who battle the rock-face in a game of strength, strategy, and cunning.

Olympic Fever
http://www.olympic.org

What's great about this web site is that you receive daily updates while the Olympics are on, plus it is a brilliant resource for the history of past Olympics the remainder of the time!

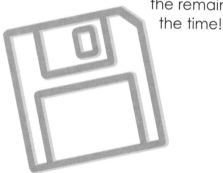

251

Cricket Voyeur
http://www.lords.org/mcc/camview/

This cricket-cam has seen some action in its day, then again, it is turned on 24 hours a day, even when it isn't the cricket season!

Fly-fishing
http://www.flyfishing.com

Pick up some of the helpful tips, and practise saying "You should have seen the size of the one I caught earlier"!

Americas Cup
http://www.americascup.org/

The biggest boat race in the world! This site captures the adrenaline and windswept excitement as it happens and, when the races are over, it contains a historical archive of the event.

Irish Racing
http://www.irish-racing.com

The Irish Times brings Irish horse racing to life at this exciting site – must be the Guinness!

Raging Bull
http://dir.yahoo.com/ recreation/sports/boxing/boxers

Not a site for the faint-hearted, this boxing site has all the latest macho action and a listing of boxing greats, both past and present.

Marathon Man
http://www.runnersworld.com

This track and athletics site features a time calculator, which may prove useful to plan how long it will take you to dash down to the bar before closing!

Checkmate!
http://www.chessed.com

Not exactly an action sport, but certainly a mind-powered one! Brush up on your moves, learn some strategies, or play against the computer guru.

Sport Drug
http://fullcoverage.yahoo.com/ full_coverage/sports/drugs_in_sports/

Whether it's a news-breaking scandal at the Olympics, or the test results of a diet supplement, you'll find the coverage and results at this fascinating site.

Top of the World
http://www.everest.mountainzone.com

A site dedicated to the mother of all
mountains – Everest – and the fearless
people who try to scale her. What is life
really like at 30,000 feet? Find out here!

Winter Olympics
http://www.winterolympics.com

Current and past information mix online
at the coolest winter sports site. Get in
touch with your inner snowman and
check out the Winter Olympics.

Golf Universe
http://www.golfuniverse.com

Think of this great site as the golfing bible – all you and your tee need to know before heading outside onto the fairways.

On Hoops
http://www.onhoops.com

These fans love basketball so much that they have set up their own web site dedicated exclusively to it. Join in the online chat, or post a message or questions.

Sports Halls
http://www.sportshalls.com/search.cfm

Every sport, in every country around the globe has a Hall of Fame tucked away somewhere – and this site is where they all meet!

Indoor Swings
http://www.cybergolf.com

No matter what the weather is like outdoors, you can play this cracking golf game anytime, anywhere!

Karate Kids
http://www.martial-arts-network.com

Every kid wants to be either Bruce Lee or the Karate Kid! Before you sign up for a martial arts class, read this – it includes a dictionary and info on how to start.

Ice Magic
http://www.aggressive.com

Excellent site for skating fans. Post your message on the bulletin board and share tips and gossip with other speed freaks.

Fun Fractions
http://www.tsoft.com/~deano

Make fractions more fun! This homework site sets out to prove that, together, math and science can be applied to basketball!

NBA
http://www.nba.com

The official site of the National Basketball Association. All the player profiles, past and present scores, and dream memorabilia for the avid collector, can be found here.

Judo Masters
http://www.judoworld.com

Judo is one of the most popular martial arts forms, so learn from the masters and find out about tournaments and download martial arts movies!

U Bet!
http://www.sportingbet.com

If you fancy a spot of cockroach racing, this site will lead you to the action, otherwise you can also check out form, hot tips, and all the info you need about online betting.

Wipe Out!
http://www.surfermag.com

The best way to get wiped out is by a wave crashing over your head whilst experiencing the exhilarating sport of surfing. This fantastic site outlines upcoming surf events and tips for beginners.

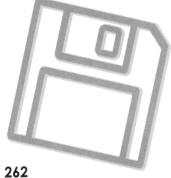

262

Hitting Trees
http://www.skinet.com

Log on to this site for step-by-step instructions on learning to ski. You'll probably fall over, but at least you'll do it like a pro!

Go to the Max
http://www.extremesports.com

Extreme, out-of-control sports for you to dream about are featured here. If you want to make the dream a reality, pull the cord...if you dare!

Fat Tyre
http://www.mbronline.com

Resource site for mountain biking
junkies. A brilliant source for facts about
mountain biking destinations, upcoming
challenges and trail information.

Ezine Ball Boy
http://www.tennis.com

Get the advantage at this regularly
updated online magazine that details
upcoming matches, tips from those in
the know, and hot player profiles.

Reservoir Dogs
http://www.discdog.com/

This cool canine site will give you hot tips on training your pooch to go one better than "Go, fetch", and actually catch a Frisbee in its mouth! Hours of fun for you both!

Back At You!
http://www.tennisserver.com

An interactive tennis site that serves up the questions and then volleys them straight at you!

Big League
http://dir.yahoo.com/
recreation/sports/coaching

A site that gives you the ins and outs on coaching a baseball team – spitting tobacco juice is optional!

NHL
http://www.nh.com

The official National Hockey League web site, where there is plenty of action and bruised shins to be viewed! Get the top info on your favorite players and chat with other fans.

Sports Store
**http://www.sportstore.com/
sportstore/default**

All your favorite sportswear ranges – and
the best bit is that you don't even have
to set foot in a department store!

Couch Potato Star
http://www.sports-gaming.com

Stay home, drink beer, play tons of
brilliant games, and become a hero
without the inconvenience of having to
get out of your comfy chair!

Euro Hockey
http://www.euroreport.com

Find the home of every European
professional hockey team – and it's all
written in English so you'll have no
trouble with translation!

Updates
http://www.dailynews.yahoo.com/
headlines/sports

Daily updated sports news by one of the
best-established search engines on the
Web. You can also run a search from
this site to any related sports topic.

Baseball Coach
http://www.he.net/~bjksz

Love baseball so much that you want to coach Little League? This excellent site gives you the step-by-step low-down on how to instruct and coach your very own team.

Big Bowl
http://www.superbowl.com

Companies don't pay eye-watering rates to place their advert near this game for nothing! Log on to the 'Superbowl' site to find out why.

269

Your Old Kitbag
http://www.kitbag.com

Do you want to be Number Eight in
your favorite team? Here you can buy
yourself the team colors and view the
latest uniforms for the season.

World Cup Fever
http://www.worldcup.com

The time of year when hundreds of
rugby fans take extended lunch breaks
to watch the games on TV! If you can't,
log on here to catch the red-hot
atmosphere.

Fantasy Football
http://www.fantasyleague.com

Join your fantasy team online and, for a small price, you can imagine being the manager of your favorite team!

Team Tracker!
http://tw-net.winsocket.com/fsearch/

Not sure where your team is playing next, or where you can find up-to-date info on them? Just visit this search engine, type in their name and find your team! Easy!

FA Premiership
http://www.fa-premier.com

The official soccer FA premiership site with tons of links, backgrounds on your favorite soccer stars, and tips from the best players in the business.

Result!
http://www.sportlive.net

If you're away on business, or prefer to see the end result of a game rather than sit through the action, you'll find the results and low-downs of each game here.

272

Davis Cup
http://www.daviscup.org

Up-to-the-minute site on the annual
Britain versus America, Davis Cup tennis
matches. It also includes an interesting
reference section about the game and
its stars.

Scrum
http://www.scrum.com

This site was voted one of the best Rugby information sites on the Web. Check out the famous quotes from the greatest of players!

Football Fetish
http://www.nflhistory.com

The history, the stars, and the scores of the NFL past and present can be found at this web site – plus a ton of trivia and fun!

Icy Action
http://www.wintersports.org

If you love having a red nose and drinking shots after a hard day on the snow, you'll enjoy this site that has all imaginable cold sports huddled in one place...tightly!

Surf the Net
http://www.surnetkids.com

Excellent, safe site for kids who want to surf the Net, but need the facts and low-down first.

Box Seats
http://www.boxing.com
'Float like a butterfly, sting like a bee' at this site that contains links to all the best boxing web pages.

Snowboarders
http://www.skicentral.com
Uncertain about where to take your board next snowboarding season? Whiz off in the right direction at this great web site that has an index of the best snow sites each season.

Rapid Rivers
http://www.wwr.u-net.com

Log on to this simple but informative site for all the information 'about racing canoes and kayaks down rapid rivers'.

It's Snow Joke
http://cnn.com/ travel/ski.report/index.html

On your next ski vacation, you'll be wanting to know what the snow coverage is like that day – this site has a direct link to CNN that will instantly answer the question.

Global Football
http://www.wqd.com/fc/gridiron

Check out some of the weird and wonderful places where people are playing football around the world right now.

Making a Racket
http://www.tennisone.com

Whether you enjoy singles, doubles, mixed doubles, or just restringing your racket, this site is a one-stop tennis bonanza.

278

Row Your Boat
**http://users.ox.ac.uk/
~quarrell/index.html**

This excellent web site is home to 'The Rowing Service', which will happily connect you to thousands of rowing links worldwide.

I'll Take Two
http://www.2-tickets.com

Click on to find very cheap tickets to worldwide sporting events, such as Formula One, NFL games and boxing matches.

279

LAGOON WEB SITE

Games, Books, Puzzles and Gizmos

Visit the Lagoon Web Site to view a staggering range of fantastic games, puzzles and books to suit all.

www.lagoongames.com

OTHER TITLES BY LAGOON BOOKS

Kids Maze Puzzle Books

Wanda the Witch and the Magical Maze
(1-902813-11-1)

Dr CK Fortune and the Lost City Labyrinth
(1-902813-12-X)

Brain-Boosting Puzzle Books

Brain-Boosting Cryptic Puzzles
(1-902813-21-9)

Brain-Boosting Visual Logic Puzzles
(1-902813-20-0)

Brain-Boosting Lateral Thinking Puzzles
(1-902813-22-7)

OTHER TITLES IN THE SERIES:

500 of the Coolest Sites for Cyberkids
ISBN: 1-902813-27-8

500 of the World's Best Web Sites
ISBN: 1-902813-30-8

500 of the Weirdest and Wackiest Web Sites
ISBN: 1-902813-29-4